D1345178

ESSENTIAL

Barbecue

p

Contents

Introduction

What is it that makes barbecuing such a favourite method of cooking? Perhaps it is the fresh air, the tantalizing aroma, or the sound of food sizzling on the rack. Whatever it is, both vegetarians and meat-lovers can enjoy cooking a variety of dishes over the coals, from marinated fish to bean curd skewers and from spicy ribs to nutty burgers. There are also many side dishes and appetizers that can be served to guests while they wait for their main course.

There are many different types of barbecues that can be bought but the simplest can be made at home from a few house bricks and a cooking rack. The most popular fuel is charcoal, although wood can also be used. Charcoal is available as lump wood, which is irregular in shape and size, but easy to light, or as briquettes, which burn for longer and with uniform heat, but are harder to light.

Light the barbecue at least an hour before you want to start cooking. The coals should be stacked and a specially designed solid or liquid barbecue lighter fuel used. Household fire lighters should not be used as they will taint the food, and kerosene and petrol are both very dangerous. The barbecue is ready to be used when the flames have died down and there is a light layer of white ash covering the coals.

Before cooking the rack should be oiled so that the food does not stick to it. For most dishes the rack should be placed about three inches above the coals, although this should be increased to four inches for poultry dishes. This will ensure that the meat is cooked through, avoiding a burnt outside and a raw inside.

There are plenty of alternatives to sausages and burgers, fish and seafood being a popular choice. When choosing fish for barbecuing a firm flesh is preferable or it may break up when turned. A firm fish, such as monkfish, is essential for skewers, and more delicate fish should be wrapped in foil and cooked in its own juices. Oily fish is especially suitable for the barbecue as it will not dry out. White fish will benefit from the addition of a paste or marinade if it is to be cooked directly over the coals.

Poultry and meat dishes can be spiced up by adding tangy tomato glazes, garlic and herbs, or spicy Asian or Mexican flavours. Marinating will help ensure a more tender meat and prevent turkey from drying out. Duck is an excellent meat to cook with as it is fatty and succulent and can be served with a variety of different flavours. Beef and lamb can both be served pink in the centre, however, pork and chicken should be skewered to check that they are cooked through – the juices should run clear.

Indonesian-style Spicy Cod

Serves 4

INGREDIENTS

4 cod steaks
1 stalk lemon grass
1 small red onion, chopped
3 cloves garlic, chopped
2 fresh red chillies, deseeded
  and chopped

1 tsp grated root (fresh)
  ginger
¼ tsp turmeric
2 tbsp butter, cut into small
  cubes
8 tbsp canned coconut milk

2 tbsp lemon juice
salt and pepper
red chillies, to garnish
  (optional)

1 Rinse the cod steaks and pat them thoroughly dry on absorbent kitchen paper.

2 Remove and discard the outer leaves from the lemon grass and thinly slice the inner section.

3 Place the lemon grass, onion, garlic, chilli, ginger and turmeric in a food processor and blend until the ingredients are finely chopped. Season with salt and pepper to taste.

4 With the processor running, add the butter, coconut milk and lemon juice and process until well blended.

5 Place the fish in a shallow, non-metallic dish. Pour over the coconut mixture and turn the fish until well coated.

6 If you have one, place the fish steaks in a hinged basket, which will make them easier to turn. Barbecue (grill) over hot coals for 15 minutes or

until the fish is cooked through, turning once. Serve garnished with red chillies, if wished.

COOK'S TIP

If you prefer a milder flavour omit the chillies altogether. For a hotter flavour do not remove the seeds from the chillies.

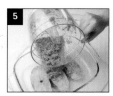

Monkfish Skewers with Courgettes (Zucchini) & Lemon

Serves 4

INGREDIENTS

450 g/1 lb monkfish tail	SAUCE:	salt
2 courgettes (zucchini)	4 tbsp olive oil	
1 lemon	2 tbsp lemon juice	TO SERVE:
12 cherry tomatoes	1 tsp chopped, fresh thyme	green salad leaves
8 bay leaves	1/2 tsp lemon pepper	fresh, crusty bread

1 Using a sharp knife, cut the monkfish into 5 cm/2 inch chunks. Cut the courgettes (zucchini) into thick slices and the lemon into wedges.

2 Thread the monkfish, courgettes (zucchini), lemon, tomatoes and bay leaves on to 4 skewers.

3 To make the basting sauce, combine the oil, lemon juice, thyme, lemon pepper and salt to taste in a small bowl.

4 Brush the basting sauce liberally all over the fish, lemon, tomatoes and bay leaves on the skewers.

5 Cook the skewers on the barbecue (grill) for about 15 minutes, basting frequently with the sauce, until the fish is cooked through.

6 Serve the kebabs with green salad leaves and warm, fresh crusty bread.

VARIATION

Use plaice (flounder) fillets instead of the monkfish, if you prefer. Allow two fillets per person, and skin and cut each fillet lengthwise into two. Roll up each piece and thread them on to the skewers.

Charred Tuna Steaks

Serves 4

INGREDIENTS

4 tuna steaks
3 tbsp soy sauce
1 tbsp Worcestershire sauce
1 tsp wholegrain mustard

1 tsp caster (superfine) sugar
1 tbsp sunflower oil
green salad, to serve

TO GARNISH:
flat-leaf parsley
lemon wedges

1 Place the tuna steaks in a shallow dish.

2 Mix together the soy sauce, Worcestershire sauce, mustard, sugar and oil in a small bowl. Pour the marinade over the tuna steaks.

3 Gently turn over the tuna steaks, using your fingers or a fork, so that they are well coated with the marinade.

4 Cover and place the tuna steaks in the refrigerator and leave to chill for up to 2 hours.

5 Barbecue (grill) the fish over hot coals for 10–15 minutes, turning once. Baste frequently with the marinade.

6 Garnish with flat-leaf parsley and lemon wedges, and serve with a fresh green salad.

COOK'S TIP

Tuna has a dark red flesh, which turns paler on cooking. Tuna has a good meaty texture, but if you are unable to obtain it, use swordfish steaks instead.

COOK'S TIP

If a marinade contains soy sauce, the marinating time should be limited, usually to 2 hours. If allowed to marinate for too long, the fish will dry out and become tough.

Salmon Yakitori

Serves 4

INGREDIENTS

350 g/12 oz chunky salmon fillet	YAKITORI SAUCE:	5 tbsp dry white wine
8 baby leeks	5 tbsp light soy sauce	3 tbsp sweet sherry
	5 tbsp fish stock	1 clove garlic, crushed
	2 tbsp caster (superfine) sugar	

1 Skin the salmon and cut the flesh into 5 cm/2 inch chunks. Trim the leeks and cut them into 5 cm/2 inch lengths.

2 Thread the salmon and leeks alternately on to 8 pre-soaked wooden skewers. Leave to chill in the refrigerator until required.

3 To make the sauce, place all of the ingredients in a small pan and heat gently, stirring, until the sugar dissolves. Bring to the boil, then reduce the heat and simmer for 2 minutes. Strain the sauce and leave to cool.

4 Pour about one-third of the sauce into a small dish and set aside to serve with the kebabs (kabobs).

5 Brush plenty of the remaining sauce over the skewers and cook directly on the rack or, if preferred, place a sheet of oiled kitchen foil on the rack and cook the salmon on that. Barbecue (grill) the skewers over hot coals for about 10 minutes, turning once. Baste frequently during cooking with the remaining sauce to prevent the fish and vegetables from drying out. Serve the kebebs (kabobs) with the reserved sauce for dipping.

COOK'S TIP

Soak the wooden skewers in cold water for at least 30 minutes to prevent them from burning during cooking. You can make the kebabs (kabobs) and sauce several hours before required and refrigerate.

Barbecued Herrings with Lemon

Serves 4

INGREDIENTS

4 herrings, cleaned
4 bay leaves
salt

1 lemon, sliced
50 g/1¾ oz unsalted butter
2 tbsp chopped, fresh parsley

½ tsp lemon pepper
fresh crusty bread, to serve

1 Season the prepared herrings inside and out with freshly ground salt to taste.

2 Place a bay leaf inside the cavity of each fish.

3 Place 4 squares of kitchen foil on the work surface and divide the lemon slices evenly among them. Place a fish on top of the lemon slices.

4 Beat the butter until softened, then mix in the parsley and lemon pepper. Dot the flavoured butter liberally all over the fish.

5 Wrap the fish tightly in the kitchen foil and barbecue (grill) over medium hot coals for 15-20 minutes or until the fish is cooked through – the flesh should be white in colour and firm to the touch (unwrap the foil to check, then wrap up the fish again).

6 Transfer the wrapped fish parcels to individual, warm serving plates.

7 Unwrap the foil parcels just before serving and serve the fish with fresh, crusty bread to mop up the deliciously flavoured cooking juices.

VARIATION

For a main course use trout instead of herring. Cook for 20–30 minutes until the flesh is firm to the touch and opaque in colour.

Herb & Garlic Prawns (Shrimp)

Serves 4

INGREDIENTS

350 g/12 oz raw prawns
(shrimp), peeled
2 tbsp chopped, fresh parsley

4 tbsp lemon juice
2 tbsp olive oil
65 g/2¼ oz butter

2 cloves garlic, chopped
salt and pepper

---

1 Place the prepared prawns (shrimp) in a shallow, non-metallic dish with the parsley, lemon juice and salt and pepper to taste. Leave the prawns (shrimp) to marinate in the herb mixture for at least 30 minutes.

2 Heat the oil and butter in a small pan with the garlic until the butter melts. Stir to mix thoroughly.

3 Remove the prawns (shrimp) from the marinade with a perforated spoon and add them to the pan containing the garlic

butter. Stir the prawns (shrimp) into the garlic butter until well coated, then thread the prawns (shrimp) on to skewers.

4 Barbecue (grill) the kebabs (kabobs) over hot coals for 5–10 minutes, turning the skewers occasionally, until the prawns (shrimp) turn pink and are cooked through. Brush the prawns (shrimp) with the remaining garlic butter during the cooking time.

5 Transfer the herb and garlic prawn (shrimp) kebabs (kabobs) to serving

plates. Drizzle over any of the remaining garlic butter and serve at once.

VARIATION

If raw prawns (shrimp) are unavailable, use cooked prawns (shrimp) but reduce the cooking time. Small cooked prawns (shrimp) can also be cooked in a kitchen foil parcel istead of on the skewers. Marinate and toss the cooked prawns (shrimp) in the garlic butter, wrap in kitchen foil and cook for about 5 minutes, shaking the parcels once or twice.

Jerk Chicken

Serves 4

INGREDIENTS

4 chicken portions
1 bunch spring onions
    (scallions), trimmed
1–2 Scotch Bonnet chillies,
    deseeded
1 garlic clove

5 cm/2 inch piece root (fresh)
    ginger, peeled and roughly
    chopped
½ tsp dried thyme
½ tsp paprika
¼ tsp ground allspice

pinch ground cinnamon
pinch ground cloves
4 tbsp white wine vinegar
3 tbsp light soy sauce
pepper

1 Rinse the chicken portions and pat them dry on absorbent kitchen paper. Place them in a shallow dish.

2 Place the spring onions (scallions), chillies, garlic, ginger, thyme, paprika, allspice, cinnamon, cloves, wine vinegar, soy sauce and pepper to taste in a food processor and process to make a smooth mixture.

3 Pour the spicy mixture over the chicken. Turn

the chicken portions over so that they are well coated in the marinade. Transfer the chicken to the refrigerator and leave to marinate for up to 24 hours.

4 Remove the chicken from the marinade and barbecue (grill) over medium hot coals for about 30 minutes, turning the chicken over and basting occasionally with any remaining marinade, until the chicken is cooked through.

5 Transfer the chicken portions to individual serving plates and serve at once.

COOK'S TIP

As Jamaican cuisine becomes increasingly popular, you will find jars of ready-made jerk marinade, which you can use when time is short. Allow the chicken to marinate for as long as possible for maximum flavour.

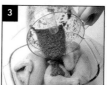

Favourite Barbecued (Grilled) Chicken

Serves 4

INGREDIENTS

8 chicken wings or 1 chicken cut into 8 portions	3 tbsp brown fruity sauce	1 tbsp olive oil
3 tbsp tomato purée (paste)	1 tbsp white wine vinegar	1 clove garlic, crushed (optional)
	1 tbsp clear honey	salad leaves, to serve

1 Remove the skin from the chicken if you want to reduce the fat in the dish.

2 To make the barbecue glaze, place the tomato purée (paste), brown fruity sauce, white wine vinegar, honey, oil and garlic in a small bowl. Stir all of the ingredients together until they are thoroughly blended.

3 Brush the barbecue (grill) glaze over the chicken and barbecue (grill) over hot coals for 15–20 minutes. Turn the chicken portions over occasionally and baste frequently with the barbecue (grill) glaze. If the chicken begins to blacken before it is cooked, raise the rack if possible or move the chicken to a cooler part of the barbecue (grill) to slow down the cooking.

4 Transfer the barbecued (grilled) chicken to warm serving plates and serve with a selection of fresh salad leaves.

VARIATION

This barbecue (grill) glaze also makes a very good baste to brush over pork chops.

COOK'S TIP

When poultry is cooked over a very hot barbecue (grill) the heat immediately seals in all of the juices, leaving the meat succulent. For this reason you must make sure that the coals are hot enough before starting to barbecue (grill).

Chicken Skewers with Lemon & Coriander (Cilantro)

Serves 4

INGREDIENTS

4 chicken breasts, skinned and boned	300 ml/½ pint/1¼ cups natural yogurt	2 tbsp chopped, fresh coriander (cilantro)
1 tsp ground coriander	1 lemon	oil for brushing
2 tsp lemon juice		salt and pepper

1 Cut the chicken into 2.5 cm/1 inch pieces and place them in a shallow, non-metallic dish.

2 Add the coriander, lemon juice, salt and pepper to taste and 4 tbsp of the yogurt to the chicken and mix together until thoroughly combined. Cover and leave to chill for at least 2 hours, preferably overnight.

3 To make the lemon yogurt, peel and finely chop the lemon, discarding any pips. Stir the lemon into the yogurt, with the fresh coriander (cilantro). Chill in the refrigerator.

4 Thread the chicken pieces on to skewers. Brush the rack with oil and barbecue (grill) over hot coals for about 15 minutes, basting with the oil.

5 Transfer the kebabs (kabobs) to warm serving plates and garnish with coriander (cilantro), lemon wedges and salad leaves. Serve with yogurt.

VARIATION

These kebabs (kabobs) are delicious served on a bed of blanched spinach, which has been seasoned with salt, pepper and nutmeg.

COOK'S TIP

Prepare the chicken the day before it is needed so that it can marinate overnight.

Chicken Satay

Serves 4

INGREDIENTS

2 chicken breasts, skinned and boned

MARINADE:
4 tbsp sunflower oil
2 cloves garlic, crushed
3 tbsp fresh, chopped coriander (cilantro)
1 tbsp caster (superfine) sugar

$\frac{1}{2}$ tsp ground cumin
$\frac{1}{2}$ tsp ground coriander
1 tbsp soy sauce
1 red or green chilli, deseeded
salt and pepper

SAUCE:
2 tbsp sunflower oil
1 small onion, chopped finely

1 red or green chilli, deseeded and chopped
$\frac{1}{2}$ tsp ground coriander
$\frac{1}{2}$ tsp ground cumin
8 tbsp peanut butter
8 tbsp chicken stock or water
1 tbsp block coconut

1 Soak 8 wooden skewers in a large, shallow dish of cold water for at least 30 minutes. This will prevent the skewers from burning on the hot grill.

2 Cut the chicken lengthwise into 8 long strips. Thread the strips of chicken, concertina-style, on to the skewers and set them aside while you make the marinade.

3 Place the ingredients for the marinade in a food processor and process until smooth.

4 Coat the chicken with the marinade paste, cover and leave to chill in the refrigerator for at least 2 hours.

5 To make the sauce, heat the oil in a small pan and fry the onion and chilli until they are

softened but not browned. Stir in the spices and cook for 1 minute. Add the remaining sauce ingredients and cook the mixture gently for 5 minutes. Keep warm.

6 Barbecue (grill) the chicken skewers over hot coals for about 10 minutes, basting with any remaining marinade. Serve immediately with the warm sauce.

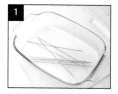

Char-grilled Turkey with Cheesy Pockets

Serves 4

INGREDIENTS

4 turkey breast pieces, each about 225 g/8 oz	4 sage leaves or $^1\!/_2$ tsp dried sage	salt and pepper
4 portions full-fat cheese (Bel Paese, grated Mozzarella or Brie or Camembert), 15 g/$^1\!/_2$ oz each	8 rashers rindless streaky bacon	TO SERVE: garlic bread
	4 tbsp olive oil	salad leaves
	2 tbsp lemon juice	cherry tomatoes

1 Carefully cut a pocket into the side of each turkey breast with a sharp knife. Open out each breast a little and season inside with salt and pepper to taste.

2 Place a portion of cheese into each pocket, spreading it a little with a knife. Tuck a sage leaf into each pocket, or sprinkle the cheese in the pocket with a little dried sage if you prefer.

3 Stretch the bacon out with the back of a knife. Wrap 2 pieces of bacon around each turkey breast, so that the pocket opening is completely covered. You can use a cocktail stick to keep the turkey and bacon in place.

4 Mix together the oil and lemon juice in a small bowl.

5 Barbecue (grill) the turkey over medium hot coals for about 10 minutes on each side, basting with the oil and lemon mixture frequently.

6 Place the garlic bread at the side of the barbecue (grill) and toast lightly.

7 Transfer the turkey to warm serving plates. Serve with the toasted garlic bread, fresh salad leaves and a few cherry tomatoes.

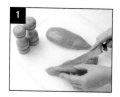

Citrus Duckling Skewers

Serves 12

INGREDIENTS

3 duckling breasts, skinned
    and boned
1 small red onion, cut into
    wedges
1 small aubergine (eggplant),
    cut into cubes

lime and lemon wedges, to
    garnish (optional)

MARINADE:
grated rind and juice of
    1 lemon
grated rind and juice of 1 lime

grated rind and juice of
    1 orange
1 clove garlic, crushed
1 tsp dried oregano
2 tbsp olive oil
dash of Tabasco sauce

1 Cut the duckling into bite-size pieces and place them in a non-metallic bowl together with the prepared red onion and aubergine (eggplant).

2 For the marinade, place the lemon, lime and orange rinds and juices, garlic, oregano, oil and Tabasco sauce in a screw-top jar and shake until mixed.

3 Pour the marinade over the duckling and vegetables and toss to coat.

Leave to marinate for 30 minutes.

4 Remove the duckling and vegetables from the marinade, reserving the marinade for basting, and thread them on to skewers.

5 Barbecue (grill) the skewers on an oiled rack over medium hot coals, turning and basting frequently with the reserved marinade, for 15-20 minutes until the meat is cooked through.

6 Serve the kebabs (kabobs) garnished with lemon and lime wedges for squeezing, if using.

COOK'S TIP

For more zing add 1 tsp of chilli sauce to the marinade. The meat can be marinated for several hours, but marinate the vegetables for only 30 minutes.

Boozy Beef Steaks

Serves 4

INGREDIENTS

4 beef steaks
4 tbsp whisky or brandy
2 tbsp soy sauce
1 tbsp dark muscovado sugar

pepper
fresh sprig of parsley, to
garnish

TO SERVE:
garlic bread
slices of tomato

1 Make a few cuts in the edge of fat on each steak. This will stop the meat curling as it cooks.

2 Place the meat in a shallow, non-metallic dish. Combine the whisky or brandy, soy sauce, sugar and pepper to taste in a small bowl, stirring until the sugar dissolves. Pour the mixture over the steak. Cover and marinate for at least 2 hours.

3 Barbecue (grill) the meat over hot coals, searing the meat over the hottest part of the barbecue

(grill) for about 2 minutes on each side.

4 Move the meat to an area with slightly less intense heat and cook for a further 4–10 minutes on each side, depending on how well done you like your steaks. Test the meat is cooked by inserting the tip of a knife into the meat – the juices will run from red when the meat is still rare, to clear as it becomes well cooked.

5 Lightly barbecue (grill) the slices of tomato for 1–2 minutes.

6 Transfer the meat and the tomatoes to warm serving plates. Garnish with a sprig of fresh parsley and serve with garlic bread.

COOK'S TIP

Choose a good quality steak, such as fillet, rump, T-bone or entrecôte, with a light marbling of fat to prevent the meat from becoming too dry as it cooks. Quick-fry steaks can also be used, but these have to be pounded with a meat mallet to flatten and tenderize the meat.

Mexican Steaks with Avocado Salsa

Serves 4

INGREDIENTS

4 beef steaks
3 tbsp sunflower oil
½ red onion, grated
1 red chilli, deseeded and
   chopped finely
1 clove garlic, crushed
1 tbsp chopped, fresh
   coriander (cilantro)

½ tsp dried oregano
1 tsp ground cumin

AVOCADO SALSA:
1 ripe avocado
grated rind and juice of 1 lime
1 tbsp sunflower oil
½ red onion, chopped finely

1 red chilli, deseeded and
   chopped finely
1 tbsp chopped, fresh
   coriander (cilantro)
salt and pepper

1 Make a few cuts in the edge of fat around each steak to prevent the meat from curling as it cooks. Place the meat in a shallow, non-metallic dish.

2 Combine the oil, onion, chilli, garlic, coriander (cilantro), oregano and cumin in a small bowl. Pour the marinade over the steaks, turning the meat so that it is well coated. Leave to marinate for 1–2 hours.

3 To make the salsa, halve the avocado and remove the stone. Peel and cut the flesh into small dice. Combine the avocado with the lime rind and juice, oil, onion, chilli, coriander (cilantro) and salt and pepper to taste and mix well. Cover and leave to chill in the refrigerator .

4 Barbecue (grill) the steaks on an oiled rack over hot coals for 6–12 minutes on each side.

5 Serve with the avocado salsa.

VARIATION

The avocado salsa can also be served with chicken. Reduce the amount of chilli if you want a milder flavour. If fresh chillies are not available, look out for jars of minced chillies, which are a good substitute.

Beef, Tomato & Olive Kebabs (Kabobs)

Serves 8

INGREDIENTS

450 g/1 lb rump or sirloin
  steak
16 cherry tomatoes
16 large green olives, pitted
focaccia bread, to serve

BASTE:
4 tbsp olive oil

1 tbsp sherry vinegar
1 clove garlic, crushed
salt and freshly ground black
  pepper

FRESH TOMATO RELISH:
1 tbsp olive oil
½ red onion, chopped finely

1 clove garlic, chopped
6 plum tomatoes, deseeded,
  skinned and chopped
2 pitted green olives, sliced
1 tbsp chopped, fresh parsley
1 tbsp lemon juice

1 Trim any fat from the beef and cut the meat into 24 evenly-sized pieces.

2 Thread the meat on to 8 skewers, alternating the meat with cherry tomatoes and olives.

3 To make the baste, combine the oil, vinegar, garlic and salt and pepper to taste in a bowl.

4 To make the relish, heat the oil in a small pan and fry the onion and garlic for 3–4 minutes until softened. Add the tomatoes and olives and cook for 2–3 minutes until the tomatoes are slightly soft. Stir in the parsley and lemon juice and season with salt and pepper to taste. Set aside and keep warm or leave to chill.

5 Barbecue (grill) the skewers on an oiled rack over hot coals for 5–10 minutes, basting and turning frequently. Serve with the tomato relish and slices of focaccia.

COOK'S TIP

The kebabs (kabobs), baste and relish can be prepared several hours in advance, to avoid any last-minute rush. For a simple meal, serve with crusty fresh bread and a mixed salad.

Kibbeh

Makes 8

INGREDIENTS

75 g/2³/₄ oz couscous	¹/₄ tsp cayenne pepper	BASTE:
1 small onion	4 tsp ground allspice	2 tbsp sunflower oil
350 g/12 oz lean minced lamb	green salad and onion rings,	2 tbsp tomato ketchup
¹/₂ tsp ground cinnamon	to serve	(catsup)

1 Place the couscous in a large bowl, cover with cold water and leave to stand for 30 minutes or until the couscous has swelled and softened. Alternatively, soak the couscous according to the instructions on the packet.

2 Drain the couscous through a sieve and squeeze out as much moisture as you can.

3 If you have a food processor, add the onion and chop finely. Add the lamb and process briefly to chop the mince further. If you do not have a processor, grate the onion before mixing with the lamb.

4 Combine the couscous, lamb and spices and mix. Divide the mixture into 8 equal sized portions. Press and shape the mixture around 8 skewers, pressing the mixture together firmly so that it holds its shape. Chill for 30 minutes.

5 To make the baste, combine the oil and ketchup (catsup).

6 Barbecue (grill) the kibbeh over hot coals for 10–15 minutes, turning and basting frequently. Serve with barbecued (grilled) onion rings and green salad leaves.

COOK'S TIP

Adding couscous to a mince mixture 'stretches' the meat, making the dish very economical to make. You can add it to other types of mince and use it to make kebabs (kabobs) or burgers.

Barbecued (Grilled) Lamb Ribs

Serves 4

INGREDIENTS

breast of lamb, about 700 g/1
  lb 9 oz
3 tbsp sweet chutney (relish)
4 tbsp tomato ketchup
  (catsup)

2 tbsp cider vinegar
2 tsp Worcestershire sauce
2 tsp mild mustard
1 tbsp light muscovado sugar

TO SERVE:
salad leaves
cherry tomatoes

1 Using a sharp knife, cut between the ribs of the breast of lamb to divide it into slightly smaller pieces.

2 Bring a large saucepan of water to the boil, add the lamb and par-cook for about 5 minutes. Remove the meat from the water and pat dry thoroughly with paper towels.

3 Combine the sweet chutney (relish), tomato ketchup (catsup), cider vinegar,

Worcestershire sauce, mustard and sugar in a shallow, non-metallic dish to make a sauce.

4 Using a sharp knife, cut the lamb into individual ribs. Add the ribs to the sauce and toss until well coated.

5 Remove the ribs from the sauce, reserving the remaining sauce for basting.

6 Barbecue (grill) the ribs over hot coals for 10-15 minutes, turning and

basting frequently with the reserved sauce.

7 Transfer the ribs to warm serving plates. Serve immediately with salad leaves and cherry tomatoes.

VARIATION

Use pork belly strips if you prefer and, as with the lamb, par-cook the pork to remove some of the excess fat from the meat.

Red Wine Lamb Skewers

Makes 4

INGREDIENTS

450 g/1 lb lean lamb
12 button onions or shallots
12 button mushrooms
salad leaves and cherry
    tomatoes, to serve

MARINADE:
150 ml/5 fl oz/²⁄₃ cup red wine
4 tbsp olive oil
2 tbsp brandy (optional)
1 onion, sliced

1 bay leaf
sprig of fresh thyme
2 sprigs fresh parsley

1 Carefully trim away any excess fat from the lamb. Cut the lamb into large pieces.

2 To make the marinade, combine the wine, oil, brandy (if using), onion, bay leaf, thyme and parsley in a non-metallic dish.

3 Add the meat to the dish and toss to coat the meat thoroughly in the marinade. Cover the dish and leave to marinate in the refrigerator for at least 2 hours or preferably overnight.

4 Bring a saucepan of water to a rolling boil, drop in the unpeeled button onions and blanch them for 3 minutes. Drain and refresh the onions under cold water, and then drain again. Trim the onions and remove their skins, which will now slip off easily.

5 Remove the meat from the marinade, reserving the liquid for basting. Thread the meat on to skewers, alternating with the button onions and mushrooms.

6 Barbecue (grill) the kebabs (kabobs) over hot coals for 8–10 minutes, turning and basting the meat and vegetables with the reserved marinade a few times.

7 Transfer the lamb kebabs (kabobs) to a warm serving plate and serve with fresh salad leaves and cherry tomatoes.

Shish Kebabs (Kabobs)

Makes 4

INGREDIENTS

450 g/1 lb lean lamb
1 red onion, cut into wedges
1 green (bell) pepper, deseeded

MARINADE:
1 onion

4 tbsp olive oil
grated rind and juice of
    ½ lemon
1 clove garlic, crushed
½ tsp dried oregano
½ tsp dried thyme

TO SERVE:
4 pitta breads
few crisp lettuce leaves,
    shredded
2 tomatoes, sliced
chilli sauce (optional)

1 Cut the lamb into large, evenly-sized chunks.

2 To make the marinade, grate the onion or chop it very finely in a food processor. Remove the juice by squeezing the onion between two plates set over a small bowl.

3 Combine the onion juice with the remaining marinade ingredients in a non-metallic dish and add the meat. Toss the meat in the marinade, cover and leave to marinate in the refrigerator for at least 2 hours or overnight.

4 Divide the onion wedges into 2. Cut the (bell) peppers into chunks.

5 Remove the meat from the marinade, reserving the liquid for basting. Thread the meat on to skewers, alternating with the onion and (bell) peppers. Barbecue (grill) for 8–10 minutes, turning and basting frequently.

6 Split open the pitta breads and fill with a little lettuce, and the meat and vegetables. Top with tomatoes and chilli sauce.

VARIATION

These kebabs (kabobs) are delicious served with saffron-flavoured rice. For easy saffron rice, simply use saffron stock cubes when cooking the rice.

Lamb Noisettes with Tomato Salsa

Serves 4

| INGREDIENTS |

8 lamb noisettes

4 basil leaves

2 tbsp olive oil

grated rind and juice of
  $\frac{1}{2}$ lime

salt and pepper

sprig of fresh basil, to garnish

green salads leaves, to serve

SALSA:

6 tomatoes

4 basil leaves

8 stuffed green olives

1 tbsp lime juice

pinch of caster (superfine)
  sugar

1 Place the lamb noisettes in a shallow, non-metallic dish. Tear the basil leaves into pieces and scatter them over the lamb.

2 Drizzle the oil and lime juice over the lamb and add the lime rind. Season with salt and pepper to taste. Cover and leave to marinate in the refrigerator for at least 1 hour or preferably overnight.

3 To make the salsa, skin the tomatoes by cutting a small cross at the stem. Drop the tomatoes into boiling water for about 30 seconds, remove with a perforated spoon and then peel off the skins.

4 Cut the tomatoes in half, then scoop out the seeds and discard them. Cut the tomato flesh into large dice. Tear the basil leaves into pieces. Chop the olives. Mix together the tomatoes, basil, olives, lime juice and sugar in a bowl and leave for at least 1 hour or until required.

5 Remove the lamb from the marinade, reserving the marinade for basting. Barbecue (grill) over hot coals for 10–15 minutes, turning once and basting with the marinade.

6 Garnish with a sprig of basil and serve with the tomato salsa and green salad leaves.

Pork & Apple Skewers with Mustard

Makes 4

INGREDIENTS

450 g/1 lb pork fillet
2 (dessert) eating apples
a little lemon juice
1 lemon

2 tsp wholegrain mustard
2 tsp Dijon mustard
2 tbsp apple or orange juice
2 tbsp sunflower oil
crusty brown bread, to serve

MUSTARD SAUCE:
1 tbsp wholegrain mustard
1 tsp Dijon mustard
6 tbsp single (light) cream

1 To make the mustard sauce, combine the mustards in a small bowl and slowly blend in the cream. Leave to stand while you prepare the pork and apple skewers.

2 Cut the pork fillet into bite-size pieces and set aside until required.

3 Core the apples, then cut them into thick wedges. Toss the apple wedges in a little lemon juice – this will prevent any discoloration. Cut the lemon into slices.

4 Thread the pork, apple and lemon slices alternately on to 4 skewers.

5 Mix together the mustards, fruit juice and oil. Brush the mixture over the kebabs (kabobs) and barbecue (grill) over hot coals for 10–15 minutes, turning and basting with the marinade.

6 Transfer the kebabs (kabobs) to warm serving plates and spoon over a little of the mustard sauce. Serve with fresh, crusty brown bread.

COOK'S TIP

There are many varieties of mustard available, including English, which is very hot, Dijon, which is milder, and wholegrain, which contains whole mustard seeds. Mustards flavoured with other ingredients, such as honey or chilli, are also available.

Spicy Pork Ribs

Serves 4-6

INGREDIENTS

900 g/2 lb pork spare ribs
150 ml/5 fl oz/²⁄₃ cup passata
   (sieved tomatoes)
2 tbsp red wine vinegar

2 tbsp dark muscovado sugar
1 clove garlic, crushed
1 tsp dried thyme
½ tsp dried rosemary

1 tsp chilli sauce
red chillies, to garnish
   (optional)
mixed salad leaves, to serve

1 If you buy the spare ribs in a single piece, carefully cut them into individual ribs using a very sharp knife.

2 Bring a large pan of water to the boil and add the ribs. Cook the ribs for 10 minutes, then drain them thoroughly. Place the ribs in a large, shallow, non-metallic dish.

3 To make the spicy sauce, combine the passata (sieved tomatoes), red wine vinegar, sugar, garlic, dried thyme, dried rosemary and chilli

sauce in a bowl until well blended.

4 Pour the sauce over the pork ribs and toss to coat on all sides. Leave to marinate for 1 hour.

5 Remove the ribs from the sauce, reserving the sauce for basting. Barbecue (grill) the ribs over hot coals for 5–10 minutes, then move them to a cooler part of the barbecue (grill). Cook the ribs for a further 15–20 minutes, turning and basting frequently with the remaining sauce.

6 Transfer the ribs to warm serving plates and garnish with the red chillies (if using). Serve with the mixed salad leaves, if wished.

COOK'S TIP

For authentic American-style ribs make sure you buy pork spare ribs and not spare rib chops. Pork spare ribs are often sold cut into individual ribs, but it is quite easy to cut between the ribs with a sharp knife if you cannot buy them already separated.

Steak & Kidney Kebabs (Kabobs)

Makes 4

| INGREDIENTS |

350 g/12 oz rump steak
2 lamb's kidneys
1 small onion, sliced
1/2 tsp dried rosemary

150 ml/5 fl oz/2/3 cup brown ale (beer)
8 button mushrooms
8 bay leaves
4 tbsp sunflower oil

TO SERVE:
cooked rice
cherry tomatoes

1 Using a sharp knife, trim the steak and cut it into evenly-sized pieces.

2 Cut the kidneys in half and remove the skin. Snip out the core and cut each kidney half into half again.

3 Place the steak and kidney pieces in a shallow, non-metallic dish.

4 Add the onions and rosemary to the dish and pour over the beer. Cover and leave to marinate in the refrigerator for at least 4 hours or preferably overnight.

5 Remove the meat from the marinade, reserving 4 tbsp of the marinade for basting.

6 Thread the steak and kidney pieces on to the skewers, alternating with the mushrooms and the bay leaves.

7 Stir the oil into the reserved marinade. Barbecue (grill) the kebabs (kabobs) over hot coals for 8–10 minutes, turning and basting with the reserved marinade. Take care not to overcook the kidneys.

8 Serve on a bed of cooked rice and with a few cherry tomatoes.

COOK'S TIP

To save time, prepare and marinate the kebabs (kabobs) a day in advance. Marinade them in a shallow dish, and turn occasionally to make sure they are completely coated.

Marinated Tofu (Bean Curd) Skewers

Serves 4

INGREDIENTS

350 g/12 oz tofu (bean curd)	slices of lemon, to garnish	1 clove garlic, crushed
1 red (bell) pepper		¹/₂ tsp fresh rosemary, chopped
1 yellow (bell) pepper	MARINADE:	¹/₂ tsp chopped, fresh thyme
2 courgettes (zucchini)	grated rind and juice of	1 tbsp walnut oil
8 button mushrooms	¹/₂ lemon	

1 To make the marinade, combine the lemon rind and juice, garlic, rosemary, thyme and oil in a shallow dish.

2 Drain the tofu (bean curd), pat it dry on kitchen paper and cut it into squares. Add to the marinade and toss to coat. Leave to marinate for 20–30 minutes.

3 Meanwhile, deseed and cut the (bell) peppers into 2.5 cm/1 inch pieces. Blanch in boiling water for 4 minutes,

refresh in cold water and drain well.

4 Using a canelle knife (or potato peeler), remove strips of peel from the courgettes (zucchini). Cut the courgette (zucchini) into 2.5 cm/1 inch chunks.

5 Remove the tofu (bean curd) from the marinade, reserving the liquid for basting. Thread the tofu (bean curd) on to 8 skewers, alternating with the (bell) peppers, courgette (zucchini) and button mushrooms.

6 Barbecue (grill) the skewers over medium hot coals for about 6 minutes, turning and basting with the marinade.

7 Transfer the skewers to warm serving plates, garnish with slices of lemon and serve.

VARIATION

For a spicy kebab (kabob), make a marinade from 1 tablespoon of curry paste, 2 tablespoons of oil and the juice of ¹/₂ lemon.

Crispy Potato Skins

Serves 4-6

INGREDIENTS

8 small baking potatoes, scrubbed
50 g/1¾ oz butter, melted
salt and pepper

OPTIONAL TOPPING:
6 spring onions (scallions), sliced

50 g/1¾ oz salami, cut into thin strips
50 g/1¾ oz grated gruyère cheese

1 Preheat the oven to 200°C/400°F/Gas Mark 6. Prick the potatoes with a fork and bake for 1 hour or until tender. Alternatively, cook in a microwave on High for 12–15 minutes.

2 Cut the potatoes in half and scoop out the flesh, leaving about 5 mm/¼ inch potato flesh lining the skin.

3 Brush inside the potato with melted butter.

4 Place the skins, cut-side down, over medium hot coals and barbecue (grill) for 10–15 minutes. Turn the potato skins over and barbecue (grill) for a further 5 minutes or until they are crispy. Take care that they do not burn.

5 Season the potato skins with salt and pepper to taste and serve while they are still warm.

6 If wished, the skins can filled with a variety of toppings. Barbecue (grill) the potato skins as above for about 10 minutes, then turn cut-side up and sprinkle with slices of spring onion (scallion), grated cheese and chopped salami. Barbecue (grill) for a further 5 minutes until the cheese begins to melt. Serve hot.

COOK'S TIP

Potato skins can be served on their own but they are delicious served with a dip. Try a spicy tomato or hummus dip.

Spicy Sweet Potato Slices

Serves 4

INGREDIENTS

450 g/1 lb sweet potatoes
2 tbsp sunflower oil

1 tsp chilli sauce
salt and pepper

1 Bring a large pan of water to the boil, add the sweet potatoes and par-boil them for 10 minutes. Drain thoroughly and transfer to a chopping board.

2 Peel the potatoes and cut them into thick slices.

3 Mix together the oil, chilli sauce and salt and pepper to taste in a small bowl.

4 Brush the spicy mixture liberally over one side of the potatoes. Place the potatoes, oil side down, over medium hot coals and barbecue (grill) for 5–6 minutes.

5 Lightly brush the tops of the potatoes with the oil, turn them over and barbecue (grill) for a further 5 minutes or until crisp and golden. Transfer the potatoes to a warm serving dish and serve.

VARIATION

For a simple spicy dip combine 150 ml/5 fl oz/ ²/₃ cup sour cream with ¹/₂ teaspoon of sugar, ¹/₂ teaspoon of Dijon mustard and salt and pepper to taste. Leave to chill until required.

COOK'S TIP

Although it is a vegetable the sweet potato is used in both sweet and savoury dishes. It is very versatile and can be boiled, roasted, fried, or cooked as here over a barbecue (grill).

Barbecued Garlic Potato Wedges

Serves 4

INGREDIENTS

3 large baking potatoes, scrubbed
4 tbsp olive oil
25 g/1 oz butter

2 garlic cloves, chopped
1 tbsp chopped, fresh rosemary
1 tbsp chopped, fresh parsley

1 tbsp chopped, fresh thyme
salt and pepper

1 Bring a large pan of water to the boil, add the potatoes and par-boil them for 10 minutes. Drain the potatoes, refresh under cold water and drain them again thoroughly.

2 Transfer the potatoes to a chopping board. When the potatoes are cold enough to handle, cut them into thick wedges, but do not remove the skins.

3 Heat the oil and butter in a small pan together with the garlic. Cook gently until the garlic begins to brown, then remove the pan from the heat.

4 Stir the herbs and salt and pepper to taste into the mixture in the pan.

5 Brush the herb mixture over the potatoes.

6 Barbecue (grill) the potatoes over hot coals for 10–15 minutes, brushing liberally with any of the remaining herb and butter mixture, or until the potatoes are just tender.

7 Transfer the barbecued garlic potatoes to a warm serving plate and serve as a starter or as a side dish.

COOK'S TIP

You may find it easier to barbecue (grill) these potatoes in a hinged rack or in a specially designed barbecue (grill) roasting tray.

Nutty Rice Burgers

Makes 6

INGREDIENTS
---

1 tbsp sunflower oil
1 small onion, chopped finely
100 g/3½ oz mushrooms,
   chopped finely
350 g/12 oz/8 cups cooked
   brown rice
100 g/3½ oz breadcrumbs
75 g/2¾ oz walnuts, chopped

1 egg
2 tbsp brown fruity sauce
dash of Tabasco sauce
salt and pepper
oil, to baste
6 individual cheese slices
   (optional)

TO SERVE:
6 sesame seed baps
slices of onion
slices of tomato
green salad leaves

---

1 Heat the oil in a pan and fry the onions for 3–4 minutes until they just begin to soften. Add the mushrooms and cook for a further 2 minutes.

2 Remove the pan from the heat and mix the rice, breadcrumbs, walnuts, egg and sauces into the vegetables. Season with salt and pepper and mix well.

3 Shape the mixture into 6 burgers, pressing the mixture together with your fingers. Leave to chill in the refrigerator for at least 30 minutes.

4 Barbecue (grill) the burgers on an oiled rack over medium coals for 5–6 minutes on each side, turning once and frequently basting with oil.

5 If liked, top the burgers with a slice of cheese 2 minutes before the end of the cooking time. Barbecue (grill) the onion and tomato slices.

6 Toast the sesame seed baps at the side of the barbecue. Serve the burgers in the baps, together with the barbecued (grilled) onions and tomatoes.

Char-grilled Mixed Vegetables

Serves 4-6

INGREDIENTS

8 baby aubergines (eggplants)
4 courgettes (zucchini)
2 red onions
4 tomatoes

salt and pepper
1 tsp balsamic vinegar, to serve

BASTE:
75 g/2¾ oz butter
2 tsp walnut oil
2 cloves garlic, chopped
4 tbsp dry white wine or cider

1 Cut the aubergines (eggplants) in half. Trim and cut the courgettes (zucchini) in half lengthwise. Thickly slice the onions and halve the tomatoes.

2 Season all of the vegetables with salt and pepper to taste.

3 To make the baste, melt the butter with the oil in a saucepan. Add the garlic and cook gently for 1–2 minutes. Remove the pan from the heat and stir in the wine or cider.

4 Add the vegetables to the pan and toss them in the baste mixture. You may need to do this in several batches to ensure that all of the vegetables are coated evenly with the baste mixture.

5 Remove the vegetables from the baste mixture, reserving any excess baste. Place the vegetables on an oiled rack over medium hot coals. Barbecue (grill) them for 15–20 minutes, basting with the reserved baste mixture and turning once or twice during cooking.

6 Transfer the vegetables to warm serving plates and serve sprinkled with balsamic vinegar.

COOK'S TIP

Use a long-handled brush for basting food on the barbecue (grill).

Pumpkin Parcels with Chilli & Lime

Serves 4

INGREDIENTS

700 g/1 lb 9oz pumpkin or
    squash
2 tbsp sunflower oil

25 g/1 oz butter
½ tsp chilli sauce
rind of 1 lime, grated

2 tsp lime juice

1 Halve the pumpkin or squash and scoop out the seeds. Rinse the seeds and reserve. Cut the pumpkin into thin wedges and peel.

2 Heat the oil and butter together in a large saucepan, stirring continuously until melted. Stir in the chilli sauce, lime rind and juice.

3 Add the pumpkin or squash and seeds to the pan and toss to coat in the flavoured butter.

4 Divide the mixture among 4 double

thickness sheets of kitchen foil. Fold over the kitchen foil to enclose the pumpkin or squash mixture.

5 Barbecue (grill) the foil parcels for 15–25 minutes or until the pumpkin or squash is tender.

6 Transfer the foil parcels to warm serving plates. Open the parcels at the table and serve at once.

VARIATION

Add 2 teaspoons of curry paste to the oil instead of the lime and chilli.

COOK'S TIP

It is a good idea to wear disposable gloves when slicing and deseeding chillies. Alternatively, rub a little oil over your fingers before you begin – the oil will help to prevent your skin absorbing the chilli juice. Wash your hands thoroughly afterwards.

Green Bean & Carrot Salad

Serves 4

INGREDIENTS

350 g/12 oz green (French) beans
225 g/8 oz carrots
1 red (bell) pepper
1 red onion

DRESSING:
2 tbsp extra virgin olive oil
1 tbsp red wine vinegar
2 tsp sun-dried tomato paste
¼ tsp caster (superfine) sugar

salt and pepper

1 Top and tail the beans and blanch them in boiling water for 4 minutes, until tender. Drain the beans and rinse under cold water until cooled. Drain again.

2 Transfer the beans to a large salad bowl.

3 Peel the carrots and cut them into thin matchsticks, using a mandolin if you have one.

4 Halve and deseed the (bell) pepper and cut the flesh into thin strips.

5 Peel the onion and cut it into thin slices.

6 Add the carrot, (bell) pepper and onion to the beans and toss to mix.

7 To make the dressing, place the oil, wine vinegar, sun-dried tomato paste, sugar and salt and pepper to taste in a screw-top jar and shake well.

8 Pour the dressing over the vegetables and serve immediately or leave to chill in the refrigerator until required.

COOK'S TIP

Use canned beans if fresh ones are unavailable. Rinse off the salty liquid and drain well. There is no need to blanch canned beans.

Spinach & Orange Salad

Serves 4-6

INGREDIENTS

225 g/8 oz baby spinach
    leaves
2 large oranges
½ red onion

DRESSING:
3 tbsp extra virgin olive oil
2 tbsp freshly squeezed
    orange juice
2 tsp lemon juice

1 tsp clear honey
½ tsp wholegrain mustard
salt and pepper

---

1 Wash the spinach leaves under cold running water and then dry them thoroughly on absorbent kitchen paper. Remove any tough stalks and tear the larger leaves into smaller pieces.

2 Slice the top and bottom off each orange with a sharp knife, then remove the peel.

3 Carefully slice between the membranes of the orange to remove the individual segments.

4 Using a sharp knife, finely chop the onion.

5 Mix together the salad leaves and orange segments and arrange in a serving dish. Scatter the chopped onion over.

6 To make the dressing, whisk together the olive oil, orange juice, lemon juice, honey, mustard and salt and pepper to taste.

7 Pour the dressing over the salad just before serving. Toss the salad well to coat the leaves with the dressing.

COOK'S TIP

Tear the spinach leaves into bite-sized pieces rather than cutting them because cutting bruises the leaves.

VARIATION

Use a mixture of spinach and watercress leaves, if you prefer a slightly more peppery flavour.

Potato Salad

Serves 4

INGREDIENTS

700 g/1 lb 9 oz tiny new potatoes	250 ml/9 fl oz/1 cup mayonnaise	TO GARNISH:
8 spring onions (scallions)	1 tsp paprika	2 tbsp chives, snipped
1 hard-boiled (hard-cooked) egg (optional)	salt and pepper	pinch of paprika

1 Bring a large pan of lightly salted water to the boil. Add the potatoes to the pan and cook for 10–15 minutes or until they are just tender.

2 Drain the potatoes in a colander and rinse them under cold running water until they are completely cold. Drain them again thoroughly. Transfer the potatoes to a mixing bowl and set aside until required.

3 Using a sharp knife, trim and slice the spring onions (scallions) thinly on the diagonal.

4 Chop the hard-boiled (hard-cooked) egg.

5 Combine the mayonnaise, paprika and salt and pepper to taste in a bowl. Pour the mixture over the potatoes.

6 Add the spring onions (scallions) and egg (if using) to the potatoes and toss together.

7 Transfer the potato salad to a serving bowl, sprinkle with snipped chives and a pinch of paprika. Cover and leave to chill in the refrigerator.

VARIATION

To make a lighter dressing, use a mixture of half mayonnaise and half natural yogurt.

VARIATION

Add cubes of cheese to the potato salad, if liked.

Tabouleh

Serves 4

INGREDIENTS

225 g/8 oz/2 cups cracked wheat

225 g/8 oz tomatoes

1 small onion

¼ cucumber

½ red (bell) pepper

4 tbsp chopped, fresh parsley

3 tbsp chopped, fresh mint

2 tbsp pine nuts

4 tbsp lemon juice

4 tbsp extra virgin olive oil

2 cloves garlic, crushed

salt and pepper

1 Place the cracked wheat in a large bowl and cover with plenty of boiling water. Leave to stand for about 30 minutes or until the grains are tender and have swelled in size.

2 Drain the wheat through a large sieve. Press down with a plate in order to remove as much water as possible. Transfer the wheat to a large bowl.

3 Cut the tomatoes in half, scoop out the seeds and discard them. Chop the flesh into fine dice. Using a sharp knife, finely chop the onion.

4 Scoop out the seeds from the cucumber and discard them. Finely dice the cucumber flesh.

5 Deseed the (bell) peppers and chop the flesh. Add the prepared vegetables to the wheat with the herbs and pine nuts. Toss until mixed.

6 Mix together the lemon juice oil, garlic and salt and pepper to taste in a small bowl.

7 Pour the mixture over the wheat and vegetables and toss together. Leave to chill in the refrigerator until required.

COOK'S TIP

This salad is best made a few hours before it is required to allow time for the flavours to develop and blend together. It can even be made a few days ahead, if wished.

Italian Mozzarella Salad

Serves 6

INGREDIENTS

200 g/7 oz baby spinach
125 g/4½ oz watercress
125 g/4½ oz Mozzarella
  cheese

225 g/8 oz cherry tomatoes
2 tsp balsamic vinegar
1½ tbsp extra virgin olive oil

salt and freshly ground black
pepper

1 Wash the spinach and watercress and drain thoroughly on absorbent kitchen paper. Remove any tough stalks. Place the spinach and watercress leaves in a serving dish.

2 Cut the Mozzarella into small pieces and scatter them over the spinach and watercress leaves.

3 Cut the cherry tomatoes in half and scatter them over the salad.

4 Sprinkle over the balsamic vinegar and oil, and season with salt and pepper to taste. Toss the mixture together to coat the leaves. Serve at once or leave to chill in the refrigerator until required.

VARIATION

Include Feta or Halloumi cheese instead of Mozzarella for a change, and use sherry vinegar instead of balsamic vinegar, if preferred.

COOK'S TIP

Mozzarella is a highly popular cheese. It is a soft, fresh cheese with a piquant flavour, traditionally made from water buffalo's milk. It is usually sold surrounded by whey to keep it moist. Buffalo milk is now scarce, and so nowadays this cheese is often made with cow's milk. Mozzarella combines well with tomatoes, and this combination is now a classic.

Pear & Roquefort Salad

Serves 4

INGREDIENTS
---

50 g/1¾ oz Roquefort cheese
150 ml/5 fl oz/⅔ cup low-fat
   natural yogurt
2 tbsp snipped chives

few leaves of lollo rosso
few leaves of radiccio
few leaves of lamb's lettuce
   (corn salad)

2 ripe pears
pepper
whole chives, to garnish

---

1 Place the cheese in a bowl and mash with a fork. Gradually blend the yogurt into the cheese to make a smooth dressing. Add the chives and season with a little pepper according to taste.

2 Tear the lollo rosso, radiccio and lamb's lettuce leaves into manageable pieces. Arrange the salad leaves on a serving platter or on individual serving plates.

3 Quarter and core the pears and then cut them into slices.

4 Arrange the pear slices over the salad leaves.

5 Drizzle the dressing over the pears and garnish with a few whole chives. Serve at once.

COOK'S TIP

Arrange the Pear and Roquefort Salad on individual plates for an attractive starter, or on one large serving platter for a side salad.

COOK'S TIP

Look out for bags of mixed salad leaves as these are generally more economical than buying lots of different leaves separately. If you are using leaves that have not been prewashed, rinse them well and dry them thoroughly on absorbent paper kitchen towels or in a salad spinner. Alternatively, wrap the leaves in a clean tea towel (dish cloth) and shake dry.

Mango & Wild Rice Salad

Serves 6

INGREDIENTS

75 g/2³⁄₄ oz/¹⁄₂ cup wild rice
150 g/5¹⁄₂ oz/1 cup Basmati
rice
3 tbsp hazelnut oil
1 tbsp sherry vinegar
1 ripe mango

3 sticks celery
75 g/2³⁄₄ oz ready-to-eat dried
apricots, chopped
75 g/2³⁄₄ oz flaked (slivered)
almonds, toasted

2 tbsp chopped, fresh
coriander (cilantro) or mint
salt and pepper
sprigs of fresh coriander
(cilantro) or mint, to
garnish

1 Cook the rice in separate saucepans in lightly salted boiling water. Cook the wild rice for 45–50 minutes and the Basmati rice for 10–12 minutes. Drain, rinse well and drain again. Place in a large bowl.

2 Mix the oil, vinegar and seasoning together. Pour the mixture over the rice and toss well.

3 Cut the mango in half lengthwise, as close to the stone as possible.

Remove and discard the stone.

4 Peel the skin from the mango and cut the flesh into slices.

5 Slice the celery thinly and add to the cooled rice with the mango, apricots, almonds and chopped herbs. Toss together and transfer to a serving dish. Garnish with sprigs of fresh herbs.

COOK'S TIP

To toast almonds, place them on a baking sheet in a preheated oven 180°C/350°F/Gas Mark 4 for 5–10 minutes. Alternatively, toast them under the grill (broiler), turning frequently and keeping a close eye on them because they will quickly burn.

This is a Parragon Book
First published in 2000

Parragon
Queen Street House
4 Queen Street
Bath BA1 1HE, UK

ISBN: 0-75253-616-8

Printed in China

Note

Cup measurements in this book are for American cups. Tablespoons are assumed to be
15 ml. Unless otherwise stated, milk is assumed to be full fat, eggs are medium and
pepper is freshly ground black pepper.